FAVOURITE
VEGETARIAN
RECIPES

compiled by
Marilyn Membery

*Illustrated with
country scenes by
Helen Allingham*

SALMON

Index

- Artichoke, Walnut and Goat's Cheese Paté 27
- Aubergine Bake 5
- Broad Bean Cannelloni 4
- Butter Bean Hotpot 7
- Carrot and Red Lentil Soup 8
- Cheese and Broccoli Pasta Puff 10
- Cheese, Onion and Herb Plait 11
- Cheese and Walnut Roast 14
- Cheese Pudding 15
- Cheesy Biscuits 16
- Cheesy Sliced Potatoes 13
- Chestnut and Red Wine Pie 18
- Courgette Bake 19
- Chick Pea Stew 21
- Glamorgan Sausages 22
- Goat's Cheese Risotto 23
- Fruit and Nut Rice Salad 24
- Lentil and Tomato Quiche 26
- Marrow, Onion and Tomato Gratin 29
- Mushroom, Lentil and Cheese Wedge 30
- Mushrooms Stuffed with Stilton 31
- Nut Roast 32
- Onion and Goat's Cheese Tarts 34
- Pumpkin Soup 35
- Quorn Fillets in Thyme Sauce 37
- Roasted Goat's Cheese Tart 39
- Roasted Tomato Sauce 38
- Sausages with Caramelised Onions 40
- Savoury Crumble 42
- Spinach Bread and Butter Bake 43
- Stuffed Aubergines 45
- Swedish Potatoes 46
- Vegetable Lasagne, Roast vegetables Lasagne 47

Cover pictures *front:* "Near Hambledon, Surrey"
back: "In Wormley Wood"
Title page: "A Sussex Cottage"

Printed and published by Dorrigo, Manchester, England © Copyright

All rights reserved. No part of this publication may be reproduced, stored in a retrieval system or transmitted, in any form or by means, electronic, mechanical, photocopying or otherwise.

A Devon Cottage near Torquay

Broad Bean Cannelloni

The first time I made this one of my guests didn't like broad beans but decided to try it. I had to give her the recipe afterwards.

- 12 cannelloni tubes
- 8 oz. broad beans, fresh or frozen
- 1 clove of garlic, crushed
- 1 quantity of tomato sauce (see page 38)
- 4 tablespoons grated Parmesan
- ¾ pint white sauce
- 1 tub of soft cheese
- Chopped fresh chives (handful)
- Nutmeg, grated

Cook the broad beans, drain and refresh with cold water. Put beans, cheese, garlic, chives and nutmeg in a food processor, season with black pepper and pulse until it is all combined but not too smooth. Put the tomato sauce in the bottom of an oven-proof dish. Fill the cannelloni with the broad bean mixture and place over the tomato. Cover with the white sauce, sprinkle with parmesan and bake at 350°F or Mark 4 for 40 minutes.

Aubergine Bake

Aubergines are delicious when cooked like this. All the individual flavours marry together but still come through when eating it.

4 aubergines   **1 whole bulb of garlic**
2 tins cherry tomatoes   **1 large ball of mozzarella**
Grated Parmesan

Slice the aubergines long ways into thick slices. Griddle or fry the slices on each side for about two minutes. Put on one side to cool. Heat the tomatoes in a pan for a few minutes. Put a slice of aubergine in the bottom of an oven-proof dish. Top with tomatoes, sliced garlic cloves, and slices of mozzarella. Continue to layer the bake until all is used. Cover with foil and bake at 350°F or Mark 4 for 40 minutes. Remove the foil for the last ten minutes. Grate the parmesan over the top and finish in the oven. Serves 2.

A cottage near Oxford

Butter Bean Hotpot

This is a simple recipe but it makes a delicious main course.

1 tin of butter beans	1 tablespoon plain flour
3 oz. broad beans (frozen)	4 oz. soft cheese
6 oz. carrots sliced thinly	6 oz. parsnips sliced thinly
1 tub cream cheese	6 oz. swede cut into cubes
1 tablespoon olive oil or butter	1¼ pints of vegetable stock

Any fresh herbs – thyme, parsley, tarragon or any you have
Black pepper to taste

Cook the vegetables (except the beans) in the vegetable stock. Just before the vegetables are cooked add the beans and heat them through. Drain the vegetables and keep them warm but keep half a pint of the stock. Heat olive oil (or melt butter if preferred), sprinkle over the flour and then gradually add the stock stirring all the time. Once you have a smooth sauce leave it to simmer gently. Whisk in the cream cheese and season with black pepper. Pour over the hot vegetables and serve with brown rice. Serves 4.

Carrot and Red Lentil Soup

This soup is a real favourite for church meals.

6 oz. onions peeled and sliced **4 oz. dried red lentils washed**
12 oz. carrots peeled and sliced **1½ pints stock (made with a stock cube is fine)**
2 teaspoons of oil

Heat the oil, and add the onions and carrots. Once softened, but not browned, add the lentils and stir well. Add the stock, stirring well. Put a lid on the pan and bring to the boil. Turn down the heat to simmer. Cook for about 45 minutes – the lentils should be soft and the soup fairly thick. Cool the mixture and then blend, adding more stock if necessary.

A cottage at Hambledon, Surrey

Cheese and Broccoli Pasta Puff

No child (or adult) will refuse to eat broccoli served like this!

**1¾ oz. butter plus extra for greasing
8 oz. mini pasta shapes
6 oz. small broccoli florets
1¾ oz. plain flour
1 pint of milk
3 oz. extra strong cheese
1 tablespoon of wholegrain mustard
3 eggs, separated
Salt and pepper**

Grease a two pint ovenproof dish. Cook the pasta and broccoli until tender. Melt the butter and stir in the flour. Add the milk and bring to the boil stirring constantly. Once thickened, stir in the mustard, add salt and pepper and simmer gently for 2 to 3 minutes. Stir in the cheese and put on one side to cool. Add the pasta, broccoli and egg yolks, stirring well. Whisk the egg whites until stiff, then fold into the pasta. Spoon the mixture into the dish and bake at 400°F or Mark 6 for 20 minutes.

Cheese, Onion and Herb Plait

This can also be served with soup instead of bread.

8 oz. self-raising flour	**1 egg**
3 oz. margarine	**¼ pint of milk**
4 oz. mature Cheddar cheese grated	**2 teaspoons of mixed herbs**
½ onion chopped finely	**Black pepper**

Sift the flour with the herbs and black pepper. Rub the fat into the flour and add the cheese and onion. Beat the egg and milk together. Add the liquid a little at a time until it forms a soft dough. Turn the dough onto a floured board and divide into three. Roll each piece into a long sausage shape, then plait the pieces together. Brush with the left-over egg and bake at 425°F or Mark 7 for 10-15 minutes. This is best eaten on the day you make it.

At Toller, Dorset

Cheesy Sliced Potatoes

This is my "comfort food" dish. I always have it with home-made sausages.

2 large potatoes, scrubbed well or peeled and sliced
1 large onion sliced thinly   4 oz. mature cheese, grated
2 eggs beaten   ½ pint of milk
1 casserole, greased lightly

Put the potatoes in the dish and layer up with onions and cheese, finishing with the cheese. Beat the eggs and stir in the milk. Strain the liquid into the casserole and bake for one hour at 350°F or Mark 4. Serves 2.

Cheese and Walnut Roast

Unusual, but certainly worth trying.

6 oz. walnuts	2 tablespoons of fresh parsley chopped
6 oz. wholemeal breadcrumbs	5 tablespoons of hot milk
3 oz. Cheddar cheese grated	½ oz. butter
1 onion grated	1 teaspoon of English mustard

Grind the nuts and add the rest of the ingredients (except the butter and milk) to the processor. Tip into a bowl and stir in the milk. Shape into a round. Grease a piece of foil and place the roast on top. Dot on the butter, wrap up the foil and bake at 350°F or Mark 4 for 40 minutes. Serve with home-made tomato sauce and vegetables. Serves 4.

Cheese Pudding

This is a really simple recipe, but served with salad it is quick, easy and tasty.

4 oz. bread   1 oz butter   2 eggs   ½ pint of milk
6 oz. grated cheese (reserve 1 oz. for later)
Black pepper   Greased oven-proof dish
I always eat brown bread but for this recipe I like to use white bread

Dice the bread and put in the dish. Warm the milk and add the butter. Beat the eggs and add the milk, cheese and pepper. Stir well and pour over the bread. I always leave this dish for at least an hour before baking. When you take it out of the oven it is all golden and puffy. Bake for 30 minutes at 375°F or Mark 5. Serve immediately. Serves 2.

Cheesy Biscuits

I like to use these when serving cheese; it is good to have home-made biscuits.

- 4 oz. wholewheat flour
- ½ teaspoon salt
- ¼ teaspoon black pepper
- A pinch of cayenne pepper
- 4 oz. mature Cheddar cheese, grated
- 4 oz. Parmesan cheese, grated
- 4 oz. butter

Sieve the flour, salt and pepper into a bowl. Add both the cheeses and rub the butter into the flour, gradually bringing the mixture together. Wrap in cling film and pop in the fridge for a few minutes. Roll out to the thickness of a £1 coin, cut with a biscuit cutter and bake on greased trays at 375°F or Mark 5 for 10-15 minutes.

At Breamore, Hampshire

Chestnut and Red Wine Pie

This makes an attractive centrepiece for Christmas Day.

**12 oz. can of unsweetened chestnut purée   1 oz. butter
2 medium onions, sliced   2 garlic cloves, crushed
2 oz. mushrooms, chopped   1 leek, finely chopped
3 fluid oz. of red wine   3 oz. white breadcrumbs
2 tablespoons of cranberry sauce
1 lb. flaky pastry   1 egg beaten for glazing**

Melt the butter in a pan and fry the onions, garlic and leeks. Add the mushrooms and continue to cook. Pour in the red wine and let it bubble away. Once it is slightly thickened, remove and stir in the breadcrumbs and chestnut purée. Roll out the pastry into two strips, one longer than the other. Put the smaller one on a greased baking tray and spoon the mixture on and carefully spread the cranberry sauce over the top. Brush the edges all the way round with cold water. Carefully put the larger piece of pastry over the top and seal well. Cut the leftover pastry into Christmas shapes to decorate the pie. Glaze with the beaten egg. Bake at 400°F or Mark 6 for 50 minutes.

Courgette Bake

Delicious and good with a green salad for lunch time.

**4 medium courgettes, washed and grated
1 onion, chopped finely
4 oz. extra strong Cheddar cheese
4 slices of vegetarian bacon grilled until brown and chopped into pieces
1 oz. butter, melted   Black pepper   3 eggs
2 large tomatoes, sliced**

Put the eggs in a large bowl and beat well. Add the other ingredients except the tomatoes. Pour into a greased oven-proof dish, top with tomatoes and bake at 350°F or Mark 4 for 35-40 minutes. Serves 2.

The Old Malt House, Brook, Surrey

Chick Pea Stew

This stew is delicious served with mashed potatoes and vegetables.

1 tin of chick peas
2 tins of chopped tomatoes
2 onions, chopped
1 garlic clove, crushed
1 red pepper, sliced
1 yellow pepper, sliced
2 aubergines, chopped
Fresh coriander to taste
1 teaspoon of oil

Heat the oil and fry the onion and garlic together. Add the aubergine and then add all the rest of the ingredients. Stir well, put in an oven-proof dish and cook in the oven at 375°F or Mark 5 for 45-60 minutes.

Glamorgan Sausages

I have tried lots of home-made sausages; a friend gave me this recipe and I cannot find a better one.

> **4 oz. wholemeal breadcrumbs**
> **6 oz. Caerphilly cheese, crumbled**
> **2 tablespoons finely chopped leeks**
> **1 teaspoon dried marjoram**
> **1 tablespoon coarse grain mustard**
> **Black pepper**
> **2 eggs (1 separated)**
>
> **Coating:**
> **2 oz. breadcrumbs (white bread if you have it, otherwise wholemeal)**
> **1 egg white**

Mix the breadcrumbs, cheese, leeks, mustard, herbs and pepper together. Bind the mixture with the whole egg and the extra egg yolk. Make into sausage shapes. Dip the sausages in the egg white and then the breadcrumbs. Put them in the fridge for about an hour before shallow frying them.

Goat's Cheese Risotto

*It took me a long while to attempt risotto but this is so simple
I enjoy making it and my family enjoy eating it!*

11 oz. risotto rice   **1 litre of vegetable stock**
1 onion, finely chopped   **1 packet of goat's cheese**
1 clove of garlic, crushed **Asparagus**
½ oz. butter

Fry the onions in the melted butter. Add the garlic and once softened add the rice, stirring well. Add a quarter of the stock and stir well. Once the stock is absorbed continue adding the stock until it is all used. Once the risotto is cooked take off the heat and add pieces of goat's cheese. Stir well and keep warm. Griddle the asparagus for two or three minutes. Serve the risotto topped with the asparagus. Serves 2.

Fruit and Nut Rice Salad

If we are having a meal at church this is something I like to take served on a pretty dish; it makes a good centrepiece.

3 oz. sultanas or large raisins
6 oz. dried fruit – apples, apricots
1 tablespoon sweet sherry
1 oz. almonds
1 oz. pine nuts

½ red pepper, deseeded and chopped
2 oz. butter
1 onion, finely chopped
Black pepper
½ teaspoon of all spice

8 oz. rice, cooked (white or brown)

Put the dried fruit in a bowl and sprinkle with the sherry. Add two tablespoons of cold water, stir well and leave to soak, stirring occasionally. When plump drain the liquid off and chop finely. Grease an oven-proof dish. Put the rest of the butter in a frying pan and fry the onion until softened. Add the rice and all the other ingredients. Put in the oven and heat through for 15 minutes at 375°F or Mark 5. This is delicious warm, but also makes a good pack-up for the next day.

Hook Hill Farm, Freshwater, Isle of Wight

Lentil and Tomato Quiche

*This is a good wholesome quiche, it can also be covered
with a pastry top and made into a pie.*

1 lb. of shortcrust pastry	1 clove of garlic, crushed
2 oz. mature Cheddar cheese	6 oz. green lentils (tinned or cooked)
1 tablespoon of oil	1 tin chopped tomatoes
2 onions, chopped	8 fluid oz. water
2 celery sticks, chopped	1 tablespoon fresh parsley, chopped

Roll out the pastry, line a flan dish and bake blind for 10-15 minutes at 400°F or Mark 6. Heat the oil and fry the onions, celery and garlic until soft. Add the tomatoes, lentils and water. Cover and simmer for 1 hour. When the mixture is thick stir in the parsley and put into the prepared flan case. Sprinkle the grated cheese over the top and bake for 15-20 minutes at 400°F or Mark 6. Serves 4.

Artichoke, Walnut and Goat's Cheese Paté

I always serve roasted peppers with this paté.

1 tin artichoke hearts   4 oz. goat's cheese
2 oz. walnuts finely chopped
3 peppers (red or yellow or a mixture of both)
2 tablespoons of oil
4 tablespoons of balsamic vinegar

Chop the artichokes until small. Mash the goat's cheese and add the artichokes and walnuts. Mix well. Put in a dish, cover and leave in the fridge until ready to serve.

Place the halved peppers under a hot grill until the skin is blackened. Put them in a polythene bag and once cooled, peel and slice into thick slices into a dish. Mix the oil and vinegar together, pour over the pepper and leave to marinate.

A Buckinghamshire House at Penn Street

Marrow, Onion and Tomato Gratin

This recipe is one my mother used to cook.

1 medium marrow	1 tablespoon of oil
2 large onions, chopped	2 teaspoons of mixed dried herbs
2 cloves of garlic, crushed	2 oz. mature cheese
1 large tin of tomatoes	2 oz. wholemeal breadcrumbs

Peel and deseed the marrow and cut into medium chunks. Heat the oil and cook the onions and garlic until softened. Add the tomatoes and marrow. Add the herbs, bring to the boil, cover and simmer. Once the marrow is cooked pour into an oven-proof dish. Mix the cheese and breadcrumbs together and sprinkle over the marrow. Put under a pre-heated grill until the breadcrumbs are golden. Serves 4.

Mushroom, Lentil and Cheese Wedge

Wonderful served hot, but leftovers make a tasty snack.

8 oz. red lentils
¾ pint of water
2 oz. mushrooms, wiped and chopped
1 large onion, peeled and chopped
1 oz. wholemeal breadcrumbs
1 oz. butter
4 oz. mature cheese, grated
1 teaspoon of dried parsley
½ teaspoon of mixed herbs
1 egg, beaten

Cook the lentils in the water until soft and all the liquid has evaporated. Melt the butter in a saucepan and fry the onions. Add the mushrooms and continue to cook. Once cooked, combine all the ingredients together and press into a greased sandwich tin. Bake in the oven at 375°F or Mark 5 for 20 minutes. I sometimes put sliced tomatoes on the top before baking. Serves 4.

Mushrooms Stuffed with Stilton

I use these as a starter when I have guests, but at home we eat them as a main course. Either way they are delicious.

4 large mushrooms
1 oz. butter
1 onion, chopped finely
2 tablespoons red wine

2 cloves of garlic, crushed
4 oz. Stilton, crumbled
2 oz. wholemeal breadcrumbs
Black pepper

Wipe the mushrooms, remove the stalks and reserve them. Grease an oven-proof tray and cook the mushrooms for five minutes. Chop the mushroom stalks. Heat the butter in a pan and cook the onions and garlic. Add the mushroom stalks and once softened add the wine and turn up the heat. Cook for a couple of minutes. Take off the heat and stir in the breadcrumbs and stilton cheese and black pepper. Cover the mushrooms with the mixture and bake in the oven at 400°F or Mark 6 for 10-15 minutes.

Nut Roast

This is the best nut roast I know of.

6 oz. brown rice, cooked	4 oz. fresh wholemeal breadcrumbs
½ oz. butter	4 oz. mixed nuts, chopped finely
1 medium onion, chopped finely	4 oz. mature cheese, grated
1 clove of crushed garlic	2 eggs, beaten well
2 carrots, grated	Black pepper
4 oz. mushrooms, chopped finely	2 lb. loaf tin, lined

Melt the butter and cook the onion, garlic, carrot and mushrooms. Stir in the breadcrumbs, nuts, rice, cheese and eggs. Season with pepper and mix well. Put in the loaf tin and bake at 350°F or Mark 4 for 1-1¼ hours.

A cottage at Roundhurst, Surrey

Onion and Goat's Cheese Tarts

I was afraid of using filo pastry, but once you try it you see how easy it is.

8 oz. pack of filo pastry	4 tablespoons balsamic vinegar
8 oz. goat's cheese	1 tablespoon brown sugar
2 oz. butter, melted	1 teaspoon dried thyme
1 lb. red onions	1 packet of rocket leaves

Cut 18 pieces of filo pastry about 6 inch square, and use to line six small bun tins. Brush each piece with a little melted butter and chill in the fridge.

Peel and slice the onions into thick slices. Fry in the oil for ten to fifteen minutes. When the onions are soft add the balsamic vinegar and sprinkle the brown sugar over. Continue to cook until almost all the liquid has evaporated and the onions have a glaze to them. Bake the tarts in the oven at 350°F or Mark 4 until golden in colour and crisp. Remove from the oven and turn the oven down to 300°F or Mark 2. Stir the rocket through the onions until it wilts, then spoon into the cases. Sprinkle a little thyme onto each tartlet and then drizzle the goat's cheese over the top and bake for about ten minutes until the cheese has melted.

Pumpkin Soup

This is a delicious, creamy soup.

1 lb. pumpkin peeled, seeded and chopped
1 medium onion, peeled and chopped
1 medium potato, peeled and chopped   1 oz. butter
3 cups of vegetable stock   1 teaspoon of brown sugar
½ teaspoon of paprika   Salt and pepper
Grated nutmeg to taste

Melt the butter and fry the onions, but do not allow them to brown. Add the potato and pumpkin and sprinkle over the sugar, mixing well. Pour in the stock and bring to the boil. Put the lid on the pan, then turn down the heat and allow to simmer for thirty minutes. Add the spice and grated nutmeg. Put in a liquidiser and serve.

The Old Tucking Mill, Bridport, Dorset

Quorn Fillets in Thyme Sauce

A delicious and creamy recipe.

4 Quorn fillets
½ **oz. butter**
1 onion, finely chopped (optional)
2 oz. mushrooms, sliced (optional)

Thyme chopped finely
1 oz. butter
1 oz. plain flour
½ **pint of milk**

¼ **pint of water**

Melt the butter and add the onions and mushrooms. Brown the fillets and put in an oven-proof dish. Wipe the frying pan, then melt 1 oz of butter. Sprinkle over the flour. Add the milk and water slowly and stir all the time until you have a smooth sauce. Stir in the thyme. Pour over the fillets and put in the oven for 20-25 minutes at 350°F or Mark 4. Serve with potatoes or vegetables, but another favourite way is to serve it on a bed of brown rice.

Roasted Tomato Sauce

This is delicious served with pasta. An excellent sauce to have in your freezer.

2 lb. red tomatoes
½ bunch of basil
2 cloves of garlic, sliced
2 tablespoons of olive oil
2 tablespoons of balsamic vinegar
Salt and pepper

Cut the tomatoes in half and put on a baking tray, cut side up. Season with salt and pepper. Sprinkle 1 tablespoon of oil over them. Dip the basil leaves in the other tablespoon of oil. Put a slice of garlic and a basil leaf on each tomato. Roast the tomatoes in the oven until the edges are blackened. Scrape all the tomatoes and the juices into a food processor. Add the vinegar and whiz together. Gently reheat the sauce.

Roasted Goat's Cheese Tart

*This looks really impressive and can be used as a starter for a dinner party.
I have made individual ones.*

1 lb. tomatoes
2 teaspoons of dried thyme
¾ lb. flaky pastry
1-2 teaspoons of oil
5 oz. goat's cheese
2 cloves of garlic, crushed
Black pepper
Greased baking tray
Fresh basil leaves

Roll the pastry into a square and put on the baking tray. Using a sharp knife, score a line all the way round about ½ an inch from the edge of the pastry, but do not cut all the way through. Put into a bowl the goat's cheese, thyme, pepper and garlic and mix together. Spread over the pastry using a flat-bladed knife. Thinly slice the tomatoes and arrange over the cheese. Season with salt and pepper. Drizzle the olive oil over the tomatoes, sprinkle with torn basil leaves and bake at 350°F or Mark 4 for 35 minutes. Serves 4.

Sausages with Caramelised Onions

This is delicious and one of my favourite recipes.

2 teaspoons of oil
2 oz. goat's cheese
1 teaspoon of demerara sugar

2 teaspoons balsamic vinegar
1 packet of vegetarian sausages
1 medium red onion, sliced finely

Heat the oil and fry the onions. Add the vinegar and boil for a minute until the liquid is like syrup. Sprinkle over the sugar and simmer gently with the mixture to become caramelised and sticky. Cook the sausages separately, then put in an oven-proof dish. Pour the onion mixture over the top and dot with goat's cheese. Put under the hot grill until the goat's cheese is melted.

Brook Lane, Witley, Surrey

Savoury Crumble

A brilliant way to introduce children to brussel sprouts!

**1 lb. potatoes, peeled and cut into 4 8 oz. leeks, sliced
1 lb. carrots, chopped 12 oz. brussel sprouts, sliced thinly
4 oz. mushrooms, sliced 1 oz. butter**

Crumble
**2 oz. plain flour 1 oz. oats 2 oz. butter 2 oz. mature cheese
2 tablespoons parsley, chopped ½ teaspoon mustard powder**

Add the potatoes to a pan of water, bring to the boil and cook for fifteen minutes. Melt the butter in a large pan. Add the leeks and carrots and cook over a low heat for two or three minutes. Add the mushrooms and cook for a further two or three minutes. Add the sliced brussels to the pan. Transfer the vegetables to a deep oven-proof dish. Once the potatoes have cooled sufficiently to handle, cut into half-inch slices and top the vegetables with these. Make the crumble by rubbing the butter into the flour and mustard powder until it is like breadcrumbs. Add the other ingredients and mix well. Sprinkle over the vegetables and bake at 375°F or Mark 5 for about 20 minutes. Serves 4.

Spinach Bread and Butter Bake

This is a really delicious savoury bread pudding. My vegetarian friends all ask me to make it when they are coming for a meal.

1 bag of spinach	4 oz. Gruyere cheese, grated
Ciabatta loaf, sliced	3 eggs
1 red onion, sliced	¾ pint milk
4 oz. mushrooms, sliced	1 teaspoon of mixed herbs

Grated nutmeg

Blanch the washed spinach, drain well and chop finely. Put the bread slices in an oven-proof greased dish. Fry the onions and the mushrooms. Add the spinach and the herbs and season well. Layer the bread and spinach mixture and half the cheese, finishing with bread. Beat the eggs and milk together and pour over the bread. Sprinkle the remaining cheese over the top. Sprinkle with nutmeg and leave for at least an hour before baking at 375°F or Mark 5 for 45 minutes.

A cottage at Pinner, Middlesex

Stuffed Aubergines

Serve these with a green salad. They are really delicious and very filling.

2 aubergines	2 oz. mushrooms, sliced
1 tablespoon of oil	6 tablespoons brown rice, cooked
1 onion, chopped	1 oz. pine nuts, roasted
2 sticks of celery, chopped	1 tablespoon of tomato purée
2 oz. cheese, grated	Salt and pepper
1 tin of tomatoes	1 clove of garlic, crushed

1 tablespoon of dried parsley

Cut the aubergines in half, put on a greased baking tray and cook for about 15 minutes. Fry the onion and garlic together. Add the celery and mushrooms, cooking until tender, and then add the rice, tinned tomatoes, tomato purée and parsley. Once the aubergines are cool, take out the flesh, chop and add to the mixture. Spoon it back into the skins and sprinkle the grated cheese over the top. Put under the grill until the cheese has melted.

Swedish Potatoes

I make this for Sunday lunch. Sometimes its amazing how many meat eaters become vegetarian when this is the meal of the day!

1 swede, sliced very thinly
1 baking potato, sliced very thinly
2 sweet potatoes, sliced very thinly
3 garlic cloves, sliced very thinly
1 large onion, sliced thinly
A couple of pinches of paprika
2 oz. wild mushrooms
5 oz. double cream
2 teaspoons of olive oil

Layer the swede and potatoes in a dish. Drizzle the olive oil over the vegetables and bake for 25 minutes at 350°F or Mark 4. Fry the onions, garlic and mushrooms together, stir in the cream and pour over the potatoes. Sprinkle the paprika over the top and cook for a further 10 minutes. Serves 4.

Vegetable Lasagne

This takes a while to prepare but is well worth it.

1 aubergine, chopped	½ bunch of basil
1 red and yellow pepper, chopped	2 red onions, peeled and quartered
1 quantity of tomato sauce (see page 38)	2 courgettes, chopped
½ pint of white sauce	9 sheets of pasta
Olive oil	Freshly grated Parmesan

Put two tablespoons of oil in a large bowl and add the chopped vegetables, mixing them round to coat them. Put on a baking tray and put them in the oven to roast until just cooked. Mix the vegetables in the tomato sauce, season with black pepper and stir in the torn basil leaves. Lightly oil the lasagne dish. Put half the white sauce on the base, then layer the lasagne and tomato filling, ending with the pasta sheets. Cover with white sauce and bake at 375°F or Mark 5 for 35-40 minutes. Once baked, grate Parmesan cheese over the top and serve. Serves 4.

METRIC CONVERSIONS

The weights, measures and oven temperatures used in the preceding recipes can be easily converted to their metric equivalents. The conversions listed below are only approximate, having been rounded up or down as may be appropriate.

Weights

Avoirdupois	**Metric**
1 oz.	just under 30 grams
4 oz. (¼ lb.)	app. 115 grams
8 oz. (½ lb.)	app. 230 grams
1 lb.	454 grams

Liquid Measures

Imperial	**Metric**
1 tablespoon (liquid only)	20 millilitres
1 fl. oz.	app. 30 millilitres
1 gill (¼ pt.)	app. 145 millilitres
½ pt.	app. 285 millilitres
1 pt.	app. 570 millilitres
1 qt.	app. 1.140 litres

Oven Temperatures

	°Fahrenheit	Gas Mark	°Celsius
Slow	300	2	150
	325	3	170
Moderate	350	4	180
	375	5	190
	400	6	200
Hot	425	7	220
	450	8	230
	475	9	240

Flour as specified in these recipes refers to plain flour unless otherwise described.

Please note, where cheese is specified in these recipes either ordinary cheese or vegetarian cheese may be used.

NICOLA PATTERNS

presents

TRIMMINGS FOR DOLLS

Decorative designs for
reproduction antique dolls
based on Victorian originals

Joan Nerini

TAFFETA PUBLICATIONS

DEDICATION

To Nicola, my granddaughter

with many thanks for her 'helping hand'
with the photographs

Text and Reproduction examples   Joan Nerini   Copyright 1995
Book/Photo Design and Illustrations   Ferini Designs, Lowestoft, Suffolk.
Photography   Paul Hobbs, Lowestoft, Suffolk.

First edition printed in Great Britain, 1995.
by Asgard Printing Services, Lowestoft, Suffolk.
for Taffeta Publications,
Brighton, East Sussex, England.

ISBN 0 9512835 3 7

All rights reserved. No part of this publication may be reproduced, stored in a retrieval system, or transmitted, in any form or by any means, electronic, mechanical, photocopying, recording or otherwise, without the prior permission of the copyright owner.

CONTENTS

Introduction		4
1.	Gathered Fabric	6
2.	Using Ribbons	9
3.	Making Bows	12
4.	Ruching and Tucks	16
5.	Using Lace	20
6.	Pleating	23
7.	Piping	27
8.	Scalloped Edges	30
9.	Colour Contrast Binding	33
10.	Cascading Folds	36
Diagrams		39/40
Stockists		40

INTRODUCTION

I started my "doll" career re-dressing original antique dolls for collectors. In order to use the correct fabric and accessories to re-create an authentic likeness to the clothes which any particular doll would have worn when new, I started to collect clothes, fabric, lace, ribbons, braid, buttons, in fact anything relating to Victorian dressmaking.

I visited textile auctions, second-hand and charity shops and spread the word amongst family and friends that I was looking for antique clothing and accessories which need not be in a perfect condition. If perfect clothing did come my way, I passed it on to a costume collector as I could not cut up a garment which was an authentic record of the social history of that period.

I kept some of the trimmings to add them to my own collection of Victorian ribbon, braid and buttons, especially those which reminded me of a decoration I had seen on original dolls clothes. Comparing the similarity of design and decoration, it is apparent that the Victorian seamstresses, who made the original doll's clothes, used their sewing skills and ideas to copy and reduce the styles and designs of adult and children's fashion of the the nineteenth century.

In this book the colour photographs show the smaller versions that I have made of some of the Victorian trimmings in my collection to demonstrate how effectively these reproductions could be used to decorate dolls' clothes. The making-up instructions are easy to follow and demonstrate how the Victorian seamstress was very skilled at creating the illusion of a complicated design with the simplest of construction.

All the fabric, lace, ribbon, etc., that I have used for these examples are obtainable today. Some of the suppliers are listed in the Stockists list on Page 40. When purchasing modern fabrics or ribbons care should be taken to choose only the more subtle colours to reflect yesteryear shades.

Each chapter covers a different technique and a colour photograph shows the antique trimmings together with the reproduction examples. The original trimming is held or identified by the gloved hand of my granddaughter, Nicola. Her slim hand easily fitted into an antique kid glove.

A doll is extending her porcelain arm and is holding or indicating the reproduction examples of the trimming with her hand. The larger doll's hand belongs to Daisy - a Dollies Galore design - and the smaller hand belongs to a reproduction antique Bru made by Stan Tomlinson. I have also used some of the trimmings described in this book to decorate the sleeves that either doll is wearing in the photographs.

Instructions on how to make up the small trimmings and how to cut out the fabric or ribbon to fit the proportions of the doll's outfit to which each trimming would be attached, are given in great detail. There are some diagrams at the end of the book to illustrate the construction of some of the trimmings where I felt a more visual explanation would be helpful.

Just a small tip -
As most trimmings seem to involve gathering, try to keep the length of thread in your needle only a little longer than the width you are gathering. Too long a thread in your needle not only weakens the thread as it is drawn continuously through the fabric but also the constant friction tends to make it knot more easily. Also your arm can become very weary because of the effort to extend it every time you draw out a long thread !

I hope you will enjoy making these trimmings and finding ways to add them to your dolls' clothes. I have included some ideas as to where the various trimmings might be used but I am sure, using your imagination and creativity, you will discover more ideas of your own.

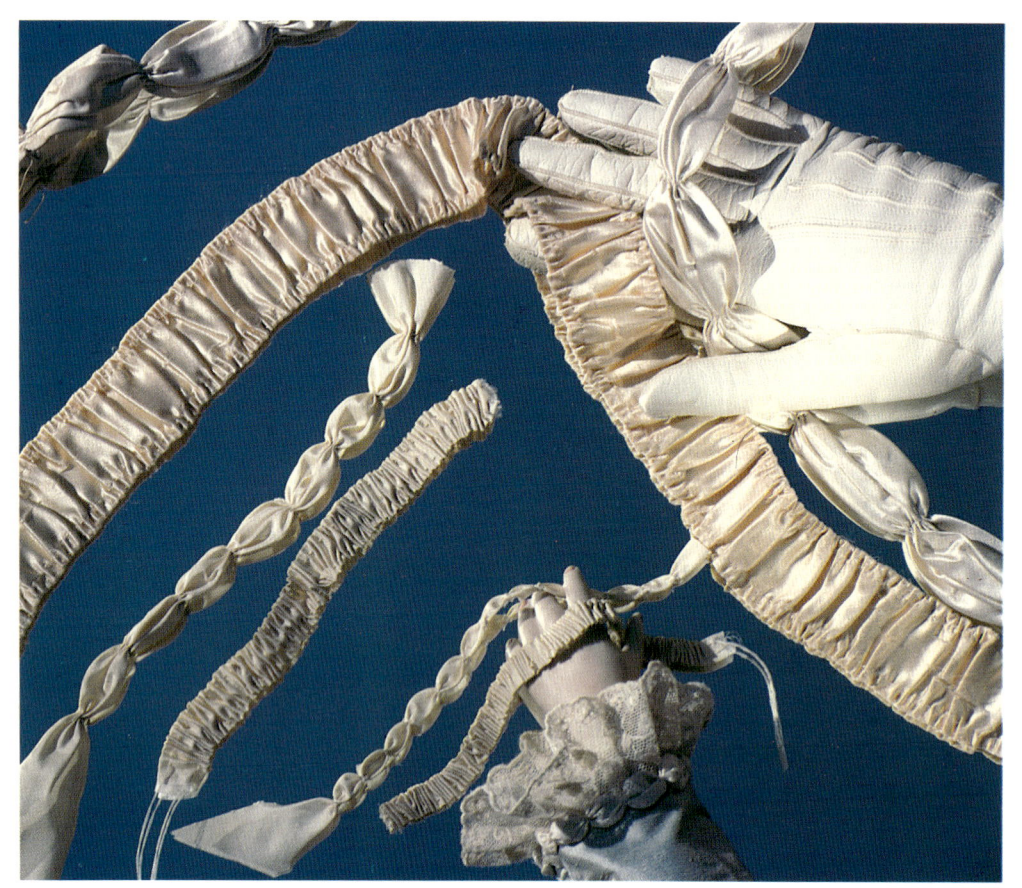

1
GATHERED FABRIC

No. 1   GATHERED FABRIC

In the photograph opposite, the antique trimmings are held in the gloved hand. The oval shaped trimming had been made from a length of bias cut silk satin, 4" (10cm) wide, and gathered at regular intervals to create rounded shapes along its length. The straight edged gathered trimming, cut on the straight of the fabric, had been gathered along each folded edge, resulting in vertical folds.

Using cream silk taffeta, I made narrow reproduction examples and even narrower ones which are held in the doll's hand. The original antique width would be more appropriate for a larger doll. The closer the gathers are drawn together, the closer the folds and consequent fullness.

Either of these trimmings could be applied to a bodice, around a neck, around the lower edge of a skirt, to sleeves with added lace - see the trimming on the doll's sleeve. Either could also be used to cover the raw edge of an applied frill, or add decoration to a hat.

For an Oval shaped trimming:
Measure the length required for the trimming and add another 2 to 3 inches (5 to 8 cm) to allow for a slight reduction when the length is gathered into sections.

Cut the required length on the bias of the fabric, and 1" wide (2.5cm), or narrower if required.

To make up:
Turn a narrow fold to wrong side along either side of length to neaten edges and press. (The side folds of the antique trimming had been left with raw edges and not hemmed down to allow the edges to curve without restriction.

Using your thread double, run vertical gathering stitches at regular intervals, the distance between gathers depending on the width of the trimming. Fasten thread firmly at start. Draw up gathers as tightly as possible. Finish thread securely before breaking off, so that gathers remain intact. When you have completed the required length, you will notice that the outer edges have curved attractively.

For a Straight gathered trimming:

The measurement required for this trimming will depend on the fullness to be achieved.

If you are in doubt about the fullness you require and the amount of fabric needed to achieve a particular fullness, prepare a 6" (15cm) length cutting the fabric the required width plus seam allowances for the folded edges. Gather and draw up fullness to the required effect. Measure the result (1 unit). For every unit of gathered measurement you will need to have 6" (15cm) of flat fabric to start with.

(Example: If the 6" (15cm) sample is drawn up to 2" (5cm) of gathers and the flat measurement to which the trimming will be attached is 36" (90cm), then :

Divide 2" into 36" = 18 times.
Multiply 18 by 6" (15cm) = 108" (270cm).

The length of fabric required will be 108" (270cm) x (the width required plus each seam allowance for folded edges).

To make up:

Cut the required length on the straight of fabric. Fold under the edges and press. Stitch a gathering line along each folded edge. Draw up the gathers to achieve the required finished length. Press the trimming firmly after gathering to set the vertical folds.

All the reproduction examples have been gathered by hand to create a slightly uneven look to the vertical folds. If the gathers are machine-stitched, the gathered folds will be more regular.

No. 2   USING RIBBONS

In the photograph on Page 11 there is a length of antique ribbon with a woven green and pink garland design. It had been shaped at intervals with mock bows. I purchased it during one of my many travels around the country.

Immediately I saw it, I thought - "How delightful"! When I examined it more closely I realised how simple it was to construct and how effective it would be as a trimming on a doll's dress.

The reproduction examples are made from three widths of ribbon - a 40mm and 13mm wide pink jacquard design and a narrow 4mm plain coloured silk which decorates the top of the cuff on the doll's white pin-tucked sleeve.

The strong contrast of green against the white sleeve emphasises the trimming whereas the soft colours of the jacquard ribbon blend attractively with the pink silk of the doll's sleeve in the photograph on Page 24.

To make up:
Select a width of ribbon which is suitable for the proportion of the doll's dress you are trimming. Mark the ribbon with pins as you work along the length following Diagram (i) on Page 39.

Fold and press the pleats in the direction of arrows. Secure each outer fold in the centre with two small invisible stitches on the right side and then secure each inner fold in the same way on the wrong side. (Note how the antique ribbon at top right of the photograph is turned to show the stitching on the wrong side of the mock bow.)

Continue folding and stitching the pleats which will form the outer edges of the mock bows along the required length. Leave an amount of ribbon flat between bows as indicated. The width of each mock bow and the amount of ribbon left flat between bows could vary according to the width of the ribbon and the effect you wish to achieve.

Next, run gathers vertically in the centre of each mock bow. Draw up gathers tightly and work thread three times around gathered centre. Fasten off securely. Press whole length of ribbon to flatten bows and gathered centres.

Suggestions for use:

a)   On a bodice with a central bow at waist, bringing ribbon diagonally to each shoulder, continuing down back of bodice to meet at waist with a final bow overlapping at centre back opening.

b)   Around lower sleeve with added lace overlapping wrist edge. (See the doll's sleeve in the photograph on Page 24).

c)   Around lower skirt, either applied straight, or curved between bows.

Ribbon has always been used extensively to decorate dolls clothes with bows of every size and shape. The antique aqua blue silk bow in the photograph on page 13 could also be made up in ribbon instead of fabric.

Lace can be highlighted with a lining of ribbon, the colour of which can tone or contrast with the main fabric to which the lace is attached. In the photograph on Page 21 there is a length of handmade lace where the antique design along the straight edge had been backed with blue ribbon, leaving the pointed edging free. One end of this lace is wound around the doll's sleeve to show how decorative this trimming can be.

Very narrow ribbon has been used to decorate and emphasise the joined lace described in Chapter 5, and shown in the photograph on Page 21. Threading ribbon into the openwork design of lace will always add decoration and colour to the simplest of dresses. It is also an easy way to gather up a lace frill and at the same time add more colour.

2
USING RIBBONS

No. 3   MAKING BOWS

Bows, in all sizes and types of construction, have always decorated dolls' clothes. I acquired the two antique bows on different occasions. I have seen the use of a knotted cord within an elaborate bow on an original antique doll's costume. A copy of the antique silk bow with its pleated strands to which little bows had been attached would enhance any delicate dress. Either of these bows could be made larger or smaller.

The green bow had been made from bias cut silk fabric. Added loops decorate the sides of the centre band. Double strands with tassles attached and a knotted cord hang from the back of the bow.

The second bow to the left had been made with very fine silk fabric in a delicate shade of aqua blue. It has a double main bow with pleated strands to which small single bows have been attached towards the bottom ends.

To reproduce the green bow, I used pale turquoise silk and narrow pale blue cord but any fine fabric could be used.

To make up: Main Bow: Cut a rectangle of fabric 3" x 2½" (7cm x 6cm). With right sides together, fold in half and stitch side edges. Refold to form a square with outer edges on the bias by bringing raw edges together diagonally with stitched side seams meeting at centre.
(See Diagram (ii) on Page 39.)
Fold one diagonal raw edge over the other and run two rows of gathers across formed square. Draw up gathers tightly and secure ends firmly to form centre of bow.

The small loops at the top and bottom of centre bow and the two hanging double strands to which tassles are attached are made with fabric rouleau lengths.
To prepare these rouleau lengths:
Cut bias length of fabric, 12" x 3/4" (30cm x 2cm) for short loops at centre bow and a bias

3
MAKING BOWS

The smaller version of the aqua blue bow is made with pink silk taffeta fabric and is attached to the doll's sleeve.

It could be made with ribbon, using 32mm wide silk ribbon for the main bows and long strands (the vertical pleating of strands would need to be made narrower), and 13mm wide matching ribbon for the small bows.

To make up in fabric:
Main double bow:
Cut two lengths :   3 ½" x 1 ¼ (9cm x 3cm) and 3" x 3/4" (7.5cm x 2cm).

With right sides together, fold each length in half and stitch seam. Draw to right side and press with seam at centre back. Overlap ends of each bow at centre back and stitch in place. Place second bow over first, matching centres. Gather up centres.

Centre band:
Cut piece: 1" x 1 ¼ " (2.5cm x 3cm).
Fold in half and stitch seam. Draw to right side and press with seam at centre back.

Place band around centre of double bows and stitch ends at centre back.

Long pleated strands:
Cut 2 equal lengths: 4" x 3" (10cm x 7.5cm). Narrow hem each side of both lengths. (The ends of the original pleated strands were left with a raw edge but they could be hemmed to neaten if preferred.) Reduce the width to ½" (1cm) with three overlapping knife pleats down each length. Overlap top ends of each pleated length and attach to centre back of double bow.

Single small bows:
Cut two equal lengths: 4" x 2" (10cm x 5cm) for bows and two equal lengths 1" x ½" (2.5cm x 1cm) for centre bands.

Make-up in the same way as larger main bow. Attach each finished bow to long pleated strands about 1" (2.5cm) up from end.

To keep the small bows from overlapping, attach a small length of narrow rouleau from bow to bow at back.

length of fabric 10" x 1" (25cm x 2.5cm) for hanging double strands.

Make-up both rouleau lengths as follows: With right sides together, stitch a ¼" (5mm) seam. Draw rouleau through to right side and press with seam at centre back.

For the top and bottom loops at centre bow: Cut the 12" (30cm) length of rouleau in half. With centre seamline facing, bring raw ends of one half length to meet at centre back and stitch across centre to form two loops. Stitch other half in the same way. Place centre of one double loop to top and the other to bottom of centre bow. Stitch in place.

To complete the bow: Cut a bias strip of fabric 1" x 1" (2.5cm x 2.5cm) for centre band. Fold band in half and stitch a ¼" (5mm) seam. Bring band to right side and press with seam at centre back. Place band around bow including attached loops. Secure at back.

For the hanging double strands: Cut the 10" (25cm) length of rouleau in half. Overlap raw ends of each half separately having seam at the back for both sides of each loop. Secure top with a few stitches and place top of both loops side by side at back of centre band of bow. Stitch in place.

Tassles: - Make 2.
Cut a piece of card, 1½" x 4" (4cm x 10cm).

Wind embroidery silk over the narrow width of card for 30 rounds. Thread a long double strand in a sewing needle and knot ends. Place needle under one end of wound silk and pass needle through double thread at end knot. Secure with a few stitches but do not cut thread. Cut the silk strands at bottom end to release tassle from card. Return to needle and wind silk several times around top to form an oval ball. Attach top of each tassle to the end of hanging strands.

Cut a 10" (25cm) length of narrow cord. Make three knots, one over the other at centre. Make another knot half way up each half of cord. Oversew top raw ends and stitch them together at back of centre bow.

4

RUCHING & TUCKS

No. 4   RUCHING AND TUCKS

The decoration on the antique pink sash which was part of a young girl's party dress is similar to the needlework used for a plastron front on a French doll's dress.

The reproduction example in cream silk taffeta copies the original sash but it could be made any length and width to suit the proportion of a doll's dress. The colour of the sash could match, tone or contrast with the main fabric. The measurement and the number of tucks to create the decoration at centre front and ruching at back edges could vary according to the size of doll.

The following instructions will make a Sash to fit a 26" to 30" (66cm to 77cm) doll.

Cut a length of silk 9" x 24" (23cm x 6lcm). Narrow hem (or roll a hem) along each side of length.
To make up:
Ruching and tucks at each end of sash:
Fold 2" (5cm) towards the wrong side and hem in place. Work 10 rows of small running stitches close together starting at stitching line of hem. Work towards sash end and leave ½" (1cm) flat at outer fold (A frilled edging will form when gathering is completed.)

Fasten each thread securely at start and leave a length free at other edge. Start each gathering row on the same side so that all the loose threads are extended on the other side. This will make the gathers easier to draw up, but before gathering up the ruching, make two tucks (measuring 1/8" (3mm) finished and 1/8" (3mm) apart) with small running stitches in the single fabric starting 1/8" (3mm) away from the hem of fold.

Taking all 10 gathering threads together, draw up ruching to measure 2" (5cm) across. Secure each thread separately. Draw up the two tucks to measure 2 ½" (6.5cm) across and fasten each thread separately. Adjust gathers evenly.

Repeat ruching and tucks for the other end.

For tucks at centre of sash:
Find the centre front of sash. Stitch an 1/8" (3mm) tuck at centre front. Make three more 1/8" (3mm) tucks each side of centre, and space them 1/8" (3mm) apart. Start each gathering thread on the same side as before. Draw up all seven threads of tucks to measure 2½" (6.5cm) across and fasten each thread separately. Adjust gathers evenly.

Pull the sash taut and press over resulting folds between the end ruching and centre tucks. The hemmed edges should be pressed towards the wrong side out of sight. To fasten sash, add 3 hooks and 3 long bar handworked loops to wrong side at end frills.

You will notice that I have used the method of gathering tucks to decorate the doll's sleeve and create a frilled cuff effect. Use a simple full sleeve pattern with an underarm seam so that you can sew the tucks on a flat area towards the wrist edge and work from the following instructions.

To make a sleeve with this decoration:
Decide on the width of the sleeve you are making and allow for the folded cuff effect in the underarm length. Omitting the side seam allowances, divide the wrist edge measurement by 3/8" (9mm) to find out how many tucks to sew. Check that the reduced sleeve width will match the width of the doll's handspan - diagonally across from little finger to thumb - and is sufficient to go over the doll's hand.

Decide on the depth of the cuff effect and measure twice this depth from the raw edge of sleeve. This is the line where you will start all the vertical tucks. Stitch each tuck, 1/8" (3mm) in width and 1/8" (3mm) apart with small running stitches for 3" (8cm), leaving each thread free. When all the tucks have been worked, draw up gathers to 1½" (4cm) and fasten each thread securely.

Stitch sleeve seam. Turn under ¼" (5mm) at end of sleeve and gather along fold. Draw up folded edge to fit at first edge of tucks on wrong side. Stitch gathered edge in place.

Applied Sleeve Ruching

In the top lefthand corner of the photograph on Page 16 there is part of an antique sleeve to which a gathered piped section has been added. This decoration could be used for a plastron front on a reproduction antique French doll's dress.

For a Plastron Front using the construction of this applied panel, make up as follows:

For base front: Decide on the width and depth to which the plastron front will be attached and cut two rectangles. With right sides together, join top and side seams. Bring front to right side through bottom open edges and press. Neaten bottom edge.

For the plastron front: Cut a rectangle of fabric on the bias, measuring twice the width and one-and-a-half times the depth of the base front. With right sides together, fold the rectangle in half and press the vertical centre fold. Place a length of narrow string into fold and stitch close to string to form a piping.

Divide each side into half again, press fold and repeat vertical channels of piping into each fold. Draw up plastron over string and adjust fullness to fit depth of base. Fold under top and bottom edges and gather along each fold. Trim and secure string. Turn under seam allowance to neaten side edges.

Divide and mark top and bottom edges of base front into four sections. Place the gathered panel over base matching the outer edges and having piping parallel to the dividing line of each section on the base. Draw up top and bottom gathers to fit.

Secure the gathered front to the base at intervals down each line of piping and around outer edges. Press the gathered front firmly and allow the fullness between piping to flatten naturally and create an antique effect.

This gathered panel could also be used for the front crown of a fitted bonnet with a flat back section, and decorated with pleated silk and lace edging at the front for a brim and a matching edging around the back neckline.

No. 5   USING LACE

The lefthand top corner of the photograph opposite shows a small part of an antique lace jacket, made entirely from lengths of insertion (straight edged) lace with an edging of matching scalloped lace. Where shaping had been necessary, small lengths had been added to create the curve of a seam or fullness of a flare.

It is often that you have kept some straight edged lace because it was too good to discard but have not used it because of its lack of length or suitability of texture or design. However, following the method of joining the edges of lace together, very popular with Victorian seamstresses, you could now use up your lace very attractively. You could even join different pieces of lace providing you match the colour and scale of design or the net background.

To make a garment in this way, place the pattern pieces before you. Follow the straight grain of the pattern arrows to establish the vertical fall of the lace. Join the lace to make a suitable rectangle to fit the pattern piece. Add smaller sections to follow any curve of a side seam. Place the lace on top of the pattern piece rather than the other way round so that you can see the vertical joins of the lace more easily. Cut out the lace pieces and reinforce any edges where the original stitching has been cut across. Make up the garment with flat seams or oversewn edges.

It may also be that you have only a short length of lace which you cannot use because the proportion is wrong. Here again the lace can be cut, joined together and used to decorate a bodice. The antique yoke in the photograph has been made in this way and could be highlighted by the colour of the bodice to which it is attached.

If one edge of lace has a definite scalloped edge or design, then this can be drawn attention to by joining the lace only where the curves meet and keeping this for the central

5
USING LACE

attraction. The narrower the lace the more delicate the trimming will be. The joined section can then be edged with the same scalloped lace drawing up fullness around any corners. Where the edging lace has been joined, the seam can be covered with narrow couched ribbon. The couching thread to hold the ribbon in place can be either a matching or contrast colour. The small example under the doll's hand shows this trimming in progress.

The antique piece of lace on the righthand side of the photograph overleaf has a centre panel of straight lace edged with a matching scalloped lace. Note the gathered corners to allow the piece of trimming to lie flat.

Remember that lace can sometimes have an extra thread which is woven into the straight edge of the lace to use as a gathering thread to draw up any fullness. Using this thread can save a lot of time especially as perhaps in the past you have not known of its existence and added a thread by hand to gather your lace.

Lace was added in profusion to garments in the Victorian era and often highlighted with colour by adding a lining of ribbon or fabric to tone or contrast with the main colour of the garment.

Cut the ribbon the same length as the lace. (Alternatively, you can use fabric which has had the cut edges oversewn.) Attach the ribbon to the wrong side just inside the edges of straight lace or to the top section of scalloped lace where the design needs to be highlighted.

Handstitching the lined lace to the main garment could prevent puckering which might occur if it were attached by machine.

A length of handmade lace has been lined with blue ribbon and is wrapped around the doll's sleeve to show how this trimming could be used.

Experiment with your pieces of lace and let your imagination and creativity do the rest.

No. 6 PLEATING

You seldom find an antique doll's costume without some form of pleating added into the design.

The antique pleated trimmings in the photograph overleaf show some of the ways to add decoration to the humble pleat.

The circular green trim has been made from a straight length of grosgrain ribbon which has been knife pleated. In order to bring the straight length into a curve, the top fold of each pleat had been placed onto the middle of the previous pleat and stitched down. This caused the outer edge to fan out and form a circle. The wider the ribbon the larger the outer curve would be.

For further decoration, the corner of the fold of each pleats at the outer edge had been drawn back and stitched to the fold of the previous pleat. See the pleated cuff on the doll's sleeve where the top edges have been pressed back but not stitched down.

In the gloved hand there is a length of antique blue ribbon which has been box pleated with a very small flat section between the folded edges of each pleat. It had been stitched through the centre of the ribbon to hold the pleats in place. This allowed the outer edges to stand away from the main fabric to which it would have been attached.

If a matching or contrast fabric is required for either of these trimmings instead of ribbon, then cut the fabric width double. Fold the length in half and stitch seam. Draw length to right side and press with seam at centre back. The length can then be pleated giving folded edges without the need to make a hem.

The antique sleeve from a lady's jacket shows two layers of knife pleats decorated with a fabric bow without tie ends. You will notice that these knife pleats are close together, falling perpendicular and in line with the

6
PLEATING

sleeve. This indicates that the fabric had been cut out on the straight and not on the bias.

The antique wide multi-coloured striped frill was attached to the bottom of an antique pink silk dress, the same colour as the pink in the stripe. Time had faded both the dress and the frill but the original bright colour remained in the dress fabric and the underside of the frill where the light had not penetrated.

There were three layers of this frill. To call it a frill is not quite correct since the centre panel was laid flat and the side pleats were not gathered but stood away from the dress because they had been cut on the bias. The edges of the side pleats had been bound with the same multi-coloured stripe fabric. Notice how the stripes have been used to create a chevron effect by cutting them in different directions on the bias. Diagram (iii) on Page 39 shows how to cut the bias strips to achieve this effect.

On Page 11 the pintucks on the doll's sleeve and cuff create the same chevron effect.

The reproduction example under the doll's hand has been made to show only one bound pleated frill attached to a flat narrower panel. This could be used in various ways:

a) at a sleeve edge.

b) over a bodice.

c) along the edges of a jacket or French style jacket bodice.

d) over armhole seams as epaulettes.

e) around a neck so that the frill becomes a downward collar.

f) around the brim of a hat.

As a double frilled panel in a smaller version of the original, it could be attached to the skirt of a fashion doll or around the peplum edge of a fitted jacket. It could also be attached down the centre front bodice of a low waisted dress.

To make a Striped Trimming with Pleated frills on either side.

You will need the following sections, cut on the bias, in width and length measurements to suit the proportion of the costume being trimmed.

Centre Panel (cut one):
  Width x Flat length to which it will be attached.

Wide Frills (cut two):
  Width x Centre Panel Length, plus extra length for layers of each pleat.)

Binding (cut two):
  Width x same length as frill.

To make up:
To bind outer edge of each frill length - fold binding in half, right sides together, and press. With right sides together, place raw edges of folded binding to raw edge of frill length and stitch ¼" (5mm) seam. Turn binding to wrong side and hem folded edge of binding along seamline. Press binding. Make narrow box pleats at regular intervals along each frill length so that finished length matches the length of centre panel. Tack pleats in place along raw edge. With right sides together, join each pleated frill to either side of centre panel. Press seams towards centre.

To hide seam, bring either side of centre panel over seam line to create a horizontal pleat towards the outer frill. When attaching trimming to main fabric, lift the fold of each horizontal pleat and handstitch through the seamline on both sides.

For a Striped Trimming with a pleated frill on one side only:

Cut a narrower flat panel and attach a similar bound pleated frill to one edge only. Turn under seam allowance along other edge of flat panel ready to attach to main fabric, or leave raw edges free to join into a seam.

No. 7   PIPING

Adding piping to a finished edge was a great favourite of the Victorian seamstress. The piping was added by hand after sections of the garment had been completed rather than encased between the seams as we would do today. The piping would be neatened on the wrong side with a facing seam. You will find that a piped edge on an elaborate original French doll's dress had been added by hand in this way.

There were times, however, when the piping would have had to be added into a seam rather than attached afterwards. One example would have been around the armhole of a fashion doll's dress. This would have been made up in the following manner:

Fold under the seam allowance around the armhole and then attach the piping by hand to extend beyond the folded edge. Gather up the sleeve head in the usual way. Place it into the armhole and adjust any fullness. Stitch the sleeve into the armhole through the stitching line of the piping by hand. This method ensures that the piping is evenly placed within the seam particularly when the armhole is very small.

The antique yellow jacket in the photograph overleaf has a double piped edge on the collar which is turned to show the finished facing on the wrong side. The puffed over-sleeves have single piped edges as well as the lower edge of the jacket. The sleeve edge shows four layers of piping. The added attraction on this antique jacket is the way the folds of the puff sleeves have been caught in the centre and again on either side with a small pleated band of yellow satin. The raw ends of the band had been folded out of sight and stitched to the undersides of the folds.

Notice the flat band across the lower sleeve to give a cuff effect. The side seam had been left open at this point for ease of dressing and closed with a button and handworked loop. It is decorated with a rosette and two

7
PIPING

leaves made from the same yellow silk - an idea to copy for a narrow sleeve on a fashion doll's jacket.

To prepare the piping for either method of construction: Measure the length of the edge to be piped. Cut a length of bias strip, 1" (2.5cm) wide and slightly longer than the required measurement. Be extra generous with this length if corners or shaped edges are to be piped. Make any necessary joins to achieve the required length. Notice a prepared length of piping beside the doll's hand, showing the right and wrong side.

Fold the bias strip in half lengthways with wrong sides together and press fold. Cut a length of narrow string and encase the string in the fold with small running stitches. Leave string extended at either end. Trim one cut edge to ta width of 1/8" (3mm). (The use of narrow string instead of the soft cordings available today allows you to stitch as close as possible to the string to create a much firmer rounded piped edge. Also very narrow string would create a piped edge more in proportion for a smaller doll's dress.

To attach the piping to a finished edge, hold the garment with the right side towards you and place the piping with the trimmed edge lying against the wrong side of garment. Keep the stitching of piping even with the finished edge of garment. With thread matching the piping, use a ladder stitch working from the stitching line of piping to the folded edge of garment and back again. After every four stitches, backstitch into the piping to prevent pulling the thread too taut and puckering the piped edge.

On the inside, turn under the facing of piping and hem, taking care not to stitch through to the right side. To join the piping ends, cut string to just inside casing. Curl fabric ends over string, tuck away into hem and fasten.

The doll's sleeve has been edged with double piping. Attach first layer and trim away facing. Attach second layer through previous stitching of first piping and hem facing of second piping to cover all cut edges.

No. 8 SCALLOPED EDGES

The length of antique narrow frill gathered over a central piping was made from yellow figured silk cut along each side edge with a special scallop cutter. This type of antique cutter not only shaped the length with scalloped edges but also indented each curve with very small scallops. This is a typical Victorian edging and can be found decorating the frills attached to many dresses of that era as well as skirt underfrills, and even the frills on underwear. So naturally this edging, being available, was added to dolls' clothes.

Today, modern pinking shears with their pointed cuts, and even the scalloped pinking shears now available, make it very difficult to re-create the cut design on the curve of each scallop.

The reproduction examples have been prepared from lengths of modern silk which have been cut on an antique cutter. The cut design differs slightly since the scallops are more pointed but the small indentations around the edges give a close representation of the antique frills. You can reduce the points of this reproduction scalloped edging by trimming across the tip with scallop edged pinking shears. See the Stockists List on Page 40 for details of where I obtained the cut silk to make this trimming which comes in two widths and also the scallop edged pinking shears. A narrow width of cut silk is shown in the centre of the photograph.

To make a Reproduction Frill of either width:
Measure the flat length to which the frill will be attached. Cut a length one and a half times this measurement using the required width of scallop edged silk. Cut a length of narrow string about 2" (5cm) longer than the flat measurement.

For a Frill with centre piping.
Fold the length of scallop edged silk in half wrong sides together. Press fold. Place string inside fold, leaving one inch extended

8
SCALLOPED EDGES

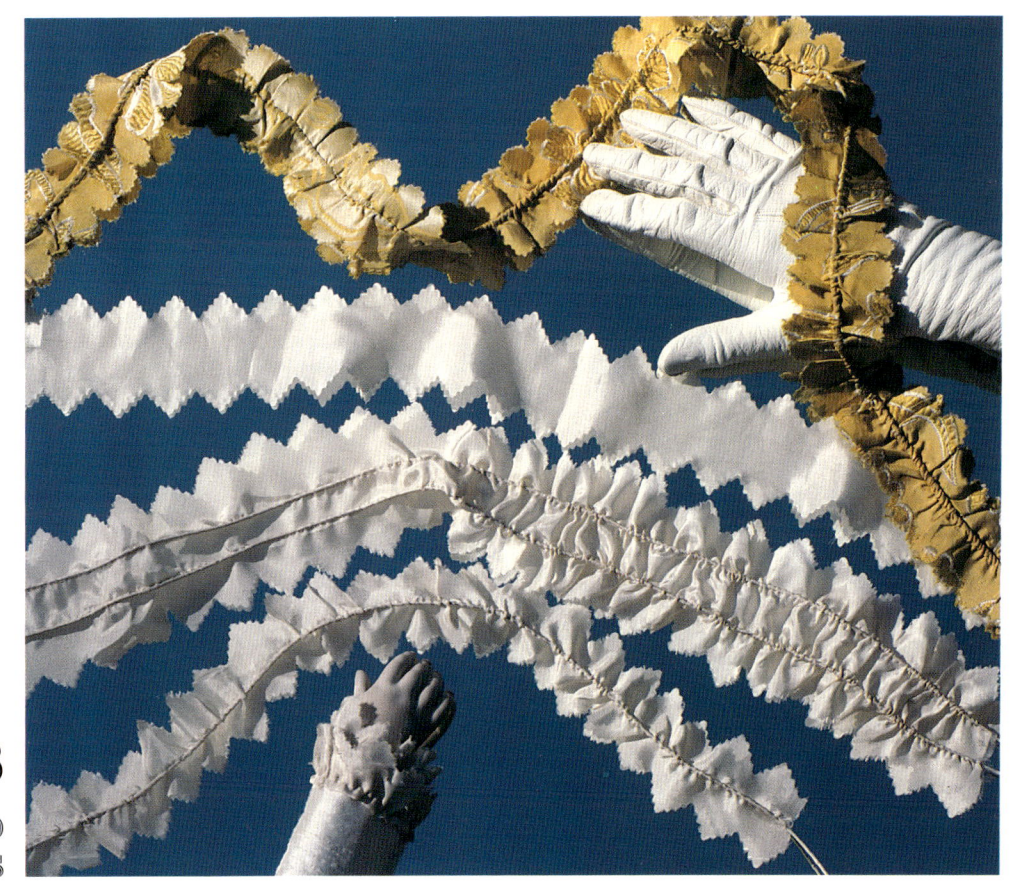

at beginning. With matching thread, stitch close up to the string with small running stitches to form a casing. (The raised piping is sewn on the right side of the fabric.) Fasten thread securely at end.

Gather the fabric over the string to fit the length required. The gathering should not be too full otherwise the beauty of the scalloped edges will be lost.

For a Frill with Double cord piping.

Use the wider scalloped lengths and gather over two parallel piping channels in the same way, creating a centre section which will gather into folds at right angles to the piping.

For a Single or Double scalloped frill (without cord piping).

The wider scalloped length can also be cut in half lengthways and used as a single edged frill. Fold the raw straight edge to the wrong side and gather over fold. For a double edged scalloped frill, do not cut length in half but fold it so that the scalloped edges fall one behind the other. Gather along fold. Adjust fullness as necessary and stitch to main fabric by hand through gathering stitches.

The doll's sleeve is decorated with a double frill in this way.

Any of these frills can be used in many ways:

a) around the lower edge of a skirt.
b) down centre front of a bodice.
c) as brettelles down each side of front and back bodice over shoulders.
d) as epaulettes over an armhole seam.
e) around the jacket edge of a French style dress.
f) attached to a wrist edge of a sleeve.
g) around waist or low waistline.

Attach the corded frills to the main fabric by stitching by hand through previous stitches of the piping. Neaten string ends as necessary.

No. 9   COLOUR CONTRAST BINDING

In the photograph overleaf there is the lower section of a Victorian skirt which shows one of the contrast bound layers of trimming attached down the front panel and a layer of bound frill around the bottom of the skirt. This contrast bound trimming was continued on the cuffs of the sleeves.

The fabric for the centre front trimming had been cut on the straight whereas the skirt frills and sleeve edging had been cut on the bias. The contrast fabric had been cut deeper than the main fabric. When attached to the top section the extra depth was arranged as a narrow bound edge at the top and a wider facing on the right side at the bottom.

The dipped V effect of the front layers was achieved by the trimming being cut longer than the width of the front panel. The centre was gathered up and the ends encased into the side seams. To make each layer lie flat against the front panel it was pulled down at the centre and stitched to hold it in place with the resulting dipped V effect.

The bias cut frills on the lower skirt and cuffs were gathered to fit the base fabric but because of the way bias cut frills flare when gathered, less length had been required than would have been needed if the gathered frills has been cut on the straight. Also the bound effect of the contrast fabric restricted the edges of the frill, creating an undulating effect.

Transferring this detail onto the cuff on the doll's sleeve is illustrated very effectively in the photograph. The doll holds a miniature version of the skirt front trimming with an added ribbon bow to emphasise the gathered centre. This trimming could be applied down the front of a waisted or low-waisted bodice or on the skirt of a fashion doll's outfit.

To make contrast edged trimmings:
Because this decoration can be made in any

9

COLOUR
CONTRAST
BINDING

size to suit the proportion of the doll being dressed, you will need to decide on the width required and also the depth of contrast needed at top and bottom of the trimming.

Experiment with a small section (about a 6" (15cm) length) to find the desired effect before cutting your fabric. Cut one example on the straight and another on the bias and notice the different results when gathered.

For a Contrast bound trimming:

Main top fabric:

Width should be the finished depth required plus seam allowances. The length will depend on the measurement required.

Contrast fabric:

Width should be the depth of top fabric plus the addition of the top and bottom colour effect required on the right side and the seam allowances to join to top fabric. The length will be the same at the top fabric.

To make up:

With right sides together, join contrast to top edge of main fabric. Press seam towards contrast fabric. Fold contrast over top of seam allowance towards the back and press top edge. Contrast will now show as a narrow bound top edge on the right side.

Fold under seam allowance along other edge of contrast. Bring contrast to right side from the back at bottom edge of main fabric. Press remaining contrast fabric over bottom edge on right side. Topstitch with matching contrast thread along the folded seam allowance to hold contrast fabric in place on the right side as a facing.

See Diagram (iv) on Page 40.

This method of adding a contrast edge could also be used to widen and decorate a plain sash, especially when you do not have enough width of main fabric to create the depth you would prefer for your sash.

No. 10   CASCADING FOLDS

I acquired the antique blue velvet decoration as an individual item so I do not know exactly where it would have been attached to the Victorian garment. The blue velvet has faded except for the inside of each fold. There you can see what a beautiful bright blue the original colour was.

The ribbon had been gathered at intervals and attached to a check ribbon as a base on which to create the cascading folds. Its unusual shape and simple construction encouraged me to copy it and, instead of the usual large bow, I attached it to the back of a French doll's dress to overhang a pleated skirt.

You will no doubt have many other ideas of how to use this attractive trimming.

As you may be unable to find the right width of velvet ribbon or the right shade of colour, I have made the reproduction example in silk fabric to show how the decoration could be made to match or contrast with the fabric of the dress. I also added a bow over the top gathered section but this could be optional.

For a reproduction trimming, suitable for a dress to fit a 15" to 19" (38cm to 48cm) doll:

Cut a piece of fabric 7" wide by 21" long (18cm x 53cm). Cut a 5" (13cm) length of 32mm wide ribbon for backing.

To make up:

Turn under a seam allowance along one cut length to neaten. Form length into a tube by placing the neatened edge over the raw edge and stitching in place. Flatten the tube by arranging the seam at centre of wrong side and pressing folds at side edges.

Run 6 rows of gathers close together at top of length. Start each row at the same side and secure each thread firmly. Leave each thread free at other side. Measure 3" (8cm)

10
CASCADING FOLDS

down from last row of gathers and work another 6 rows of gathers as before. Continue to work a further 3 sets of gathers in the same manner.

Starting at the top section of gathers, take two threads at a time and draw up fullness as tightly as possible taking care not to break threads. Repeat with the other threads of this top section. The gathering should match the width of the backing ribbon. Knot the threads together, two at a time.

Repeat for each following section of gathers.

Turn under seam allowance at top and bottom of ribbon backing to neaten.

Place the top gathered section at the top of ribbon backing and stitch in place along top, down each side (tucking in knots) and along bottom row of gathers.

Fold the flat 3" (8cm) section between the gathers towards the ribbon backing and place the wrong side of the next gathered section onto the backing ribbon, half inch away from previous gathers. Stitch in place as before.

Repeat each following gathered section in the same way. The last fold will fall below the ribbon backing.

Secure each hanging fold to the next fold with a few stitches in the centre between the folds out of sight. If the top gathered section is to be hidden then make a bow with the same fabric and attach at top.

DIAGRAMS

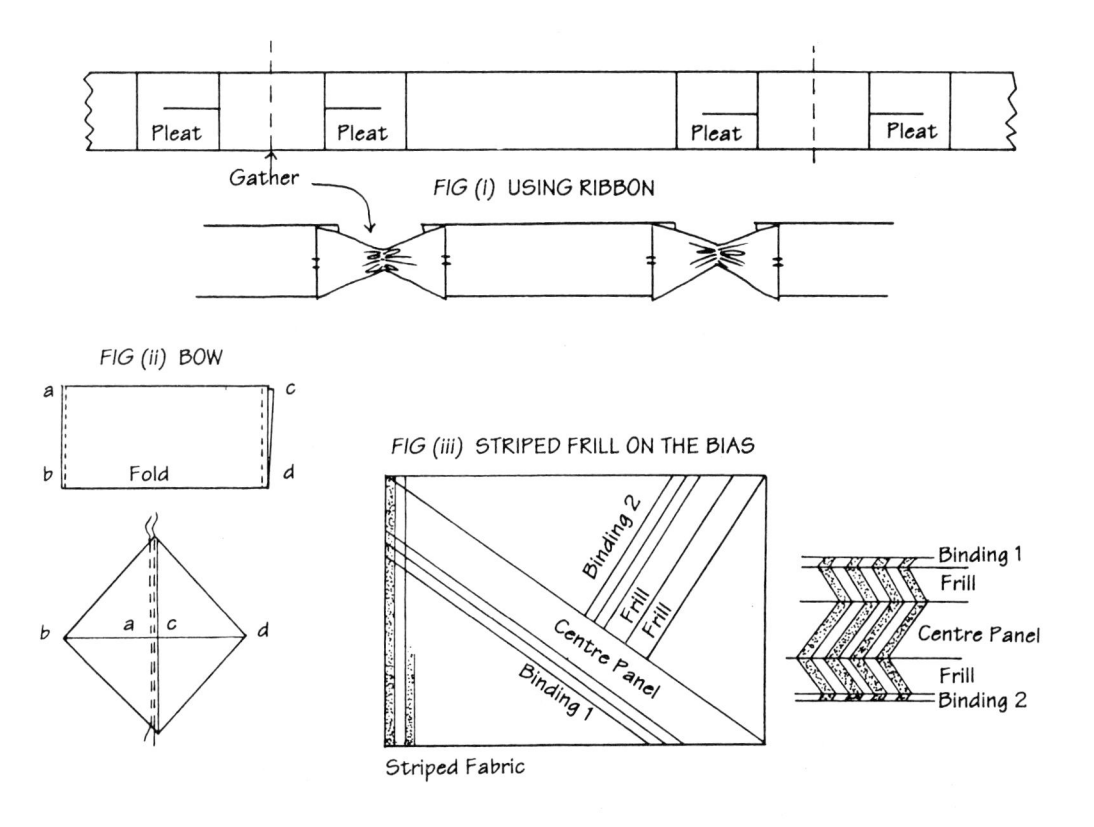

FIG (i) USING RIBBON

Pleat · Gather · Pleat · Pleat · Pleat

FIG (ii) BOW

a — c
b Fold d

b — a c — d

FIG (iii) STRIPED FRILL ON THE BIAS

Binding 2
Frill
Centre Panel
Binding 1

Striped Fabric

Binding 1
Frill
Centre Panel
Frill
Binding 2

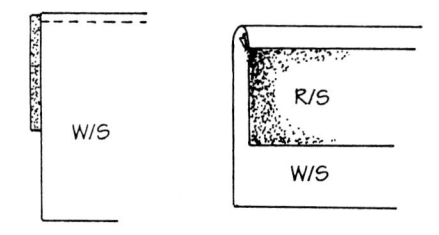

FIG (iV) CONTRAST BINDING

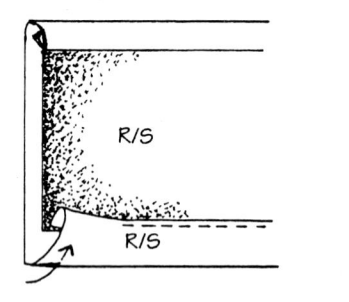

STOCKISTS

Heirloom Haberdashery including Ribbons available from:

Linda Taylor Exclusives
P O Box 51
Hartlepool, Cleveland
TS26 0YJ, England.
(Catalogue available)

Scalloped edged fine silk available in pale cream only.
In two widths. Minimum order: 5 yards.
Enquiries to:
The Dixie Collection
4 Coney Hall Parade
Kingsway, Coney Hall
West Wickham, Kent
BR4 9JB, England.
(Catalogue available)

Scallop Pinking Shears available from:

Recollect Studios
The Old School House
London Road,
Sayers Common, West Sussex
BN6 9HX, England.
(Catalogue available)